...ay in the ...

Bill laughs. 'Students! You're lucky.

'Yes, but van drivers are lucky too. Look at you. Yo... ...
got a very good assistant.'

'Oh,' Bill says. 'And what do the girls think about you?
Do they like you too?'

Mike laughs. 'I don't know.'

Bill laughs too. 'We're going to Morgan's now. Mr Morgan's daughter, Jennifer, is always in the shop. We can ask her.'

Bill and Mike drive to Morgan's shop. They take boxes from the van and go into the shop. Mike walks across the shop with three boxes. The boxes are big, and he can't see well. But he can see a girl – a beautiful girl. She is standing behind the counter. Mike smiles at her, but she doesn't smile at him.

'Stop!' she says. But Mike doesn't stop. There are some cans on the counter, and he walks into them – CRASH!

The girl runs to him. 'Oh!' she says. 'Are you OK?'

'Yes, thanks,' Mike says. He is sitting on the floor with the cans and boxes. He looks up at her. Now she smiles, and Mike smiles. She laughs, and he laughs too. Bill and Mr Morgan come from the back of the shop.

'This is Mike,' Bill says to Mr Morgan and Jennifer. 'He's my new assistant.'

'New? I can see that!' Mr Morgan says.

Jennifer helps Mike with the cans.

'Let's go now, Mike,' Bill says.

'Are you going to come again next week?' Jennifer asks Mike.

Mike smiles. 'Yes,' he says.

'Don't walk into the cans next week,' Jennifer says, and she laughs again.

Monday comes, and Bill says, 'We're going to Morgan's this afternoon. You can see your girlfriend.'

Mike says, 'Jennifer? She isn't my girlfriend. But she's got beautiful eyes and beautiful hair.' Bill smiles.

They go to Morgan's in the afternoon, and Jennifer is there again.

'You're right, Mike,' Bill says. 'Jennifer *has* got beautiful eyes! And Mike likes your hair,' Bill says to Jennifer.

Jennifer looks at Mike. His face is red. 'Lucky me!' she says, and she laughs.

Mike can't look at her. 'Bill, I can't find those cans of cheese,' he says.

4

'Cans of cheese? What cans of cheese?'

'The cans of cheese for Morgan's,' Mike says. 'I can't find them.'

'Mike, we don't have cheese for Morgan's. We have *peas* – cans of *peas*.'

Bill and Jennifer laugh again. Mike goes to the van and comes in again with the peas.

He puts the box on the counter. 'Here are your peas,' he says to Jennifer. His face is red again.

Jennifer smiles at him. 'Thank you,' she says. She has a beautiful smile.

Then a woman comes into the shop. Jennifer says, 'Hello, Mrs Smith,' and helps her.

'Let's go, Mike,' Bill says.

Mike wants to talk to Jennifer, but she is talking to Mrs Smith. He goes to the van with Bill.

'She likes you,' Bill says. 'Now what are you going to do?'

Mike thinks about this. Then he smiles. 'Next Monday I'm going to go into the shop and say, "Jennifer, can you come to the cinema with me?"'

Bill smiles. 'Good,' he says.

Monday comes again. Mike is happy. Today he is going to see Jennifer. But there is one problem. Mr Morgan and Bill are going to be there too.

They arrive at Morgan's. Mike runs into the shop, but he doesn't see Jennifer. She isn't there!

'Is your daughter here today, Mr Morgan?' Mike asks.

'Jennifer? No, my sister's ill and Jennifer is helping her today.'

They go to the van. Bill looks at Mike. Mike is smiling!

'Are you OK?' Bill asks.

'What do you mean?'

'You can't ask Jennifer to the cinema – but you're smiling!'

'I *can* ask her – tomorrow. I'm going to telephone her.' Mike is smiling because he can talk to Jennifer on the telephone. Bill and Mr Morgan aren't going to listen.

Mike telephones the next afternoon and Jennifer answers.

'Hello, Jennifer! This is Mike. Listen, *Casablanca* is at Cinema One this Friday,' Mike says. 'Can you come with me?'

'Yes, Mike,' Jennifer says. 'Thank you.'

'Hmm! – *You're* happy,' Bill says to Mike later that day.

'I'm going to the cinema with Jennifer.'

'Good.'

'Good? *Very* good! She's beautiful, and I'm going to the cinema with her!' He laughs.

Friday evening comes, but now Mike isn't laughing. He is in the van with Bill, and they aren't moving. No cars or buses in the street are moving.

'Oh, no,' Mike says, 'I'm late! I'm meeting Jennifer at 8.00.'

At 7.30 Mike runs into his house. He goes to his room and puts on clean trousers and a clean shirt. He runs to the bus stop. He is late, but the bus can take him to Cinema One quickly.

The bus comes, and he looks for his money. He can't find it!

'Oh, no!' Mike says. 'My money is in my old trousers!'

His old trousers are in his bedroom. Mike runs to his house, but the house is dark. His mother and father aren't there! Mike has a key for the front door, but his key is in his old trousers too. He can't open the door.

He goes to the back of the house. The back door is closed, but he sees an open window. There is a drainpipe near it.

Mike climbs up the drainpipe. He climbs through the window into his bedroom. His shirt isn't clean now. He puts on a clean shirt. He takes his money and his keys from his old trousers.

A police car stops in the street in front of Mike's house. 'That's the house,' one of the policemen says.

The front door opens, and they see Mike. He doesn't see them. He runs to the bus stop.

'That's the man!' the policeman says. He drives the police car to the bus stop. 'Stop!' he says to Mike. 'You're coming with us to the police station!'

The policemen take Mike to the police station. There they ask him, 'Do you often climb through windows into houses?'

'No,' Mike tells them, 'and I don't often climb through the window of that house. I live there. It's my house.'

But the policemen ask a lot of questions. Mike tells them his story again and again. Then the policemen say, 'OK, you can go. But don't climb into a house again. People see you and then there's a problem.'

One of the policemen smiles. 'Come with me in the police car,' he says. 'I can take you into town.'

Mike goes in the car with the policeman. He is very late, and Jennifer isn't at the cinema. 'She's going to be angry with me,' he thinks.

The next day Mike telephones the shop. Mr Morgan answers. Mike asks, 'Can I talk to Jennifer?'

'I'm sorry, Mike, but Jennifer doesn't want to talk to you.'

That afternoon Mike telephones again,

and Mr Morgan answers again. Mike thinks quickly. Then he says in a girl's voice, 'Hello. Is Jennifer there, please?'

'Yes. Who is this?' Mr Morgan asks.

Mike doesn't think. 'Mike,' he says. 'No, no!' he says in a girl's voice again. 'Mary. It's Mary.'

'Mike, stop this,' Mr Morgan says. 'Jennifer doesn't want to talk to you.'

On Sunday night Mike writes to Jennifer. He tells her about the money and the key in his old trousers. He tells her about his climb up the drainpipe. He tells her about the policemen.

'I'm sorry,' his letter says. 'Can we start again? I'm going to be at the Broadway Coffee House this evening at 8.00. Can you meet me there? Please!'

On Monday he takes the letter to the shop with Bill. Jennifer is there, but she doesn't look at Mike. She goes into the back of the shop. Mike puts the letter on the counter.

'She isn't going to read it,' he thinks. 'This job stops in two weeks. And then I'm never going to see her again.'

That evening Mike looks through the window of the Broadway Coffee House. Jennifer is there!

Mike goes into the coffee house. He walks across the room to Jennifer's table. She looks at him and smiles.

'Hello,' she says. 'You're late.'

'What do you mean?' Mike says. 'It's only 7.45.'

'You're *three days* late.'

'Oh – yes. I'm sorry, Jennifer.'

'No, Mike. *I'm* sorry.'

Mike sits down and looks at her. 'I'm here now,' he says.

'Lucky me!' Jennifer says.

Mike looks into her eyes. 'And *you're* here.'

'Lucky you!'

And the two lucky young people sit there and are happy.

ACTIVITIES

Before you read

1 Look at the pictures in the book. What is the story about?
   a Find these in the pictures. Look in your dictionary.
      box   can   counter   drainpipe   van
   b Look for the young man. What is he *climbing*?
      Who is he *laughing* with?
2 Answer these questions. Find the words in *italics* in your dictionary.
   a Does an *assistant help* people?
   b Are *cheese* and *peas* food?
   c Can you see a person's *voice*?
   d Do you open a door with a *key*?
   e Is a *lucky* person an unhappy person?
   f Are new shirts *clean*?
   g Is *next* month February?
   h Does this book *tell* a story?
   i Can you can walk *through* a closed door?
   j Do *trousers* have legs?

After you read

3 Why does Mike:
   a work with Bill?   **c** go to a police station?
   b visit Morgan's shop?   **d** speak with a girl's voice?
4 Mike has some big problems in the story. What are they?
   Talk about them.

Writing

5 You are Jennifer's friend. She telephones you after her visit to
   Cinema One. What does she say? Write it.
6 What is Mike going to do after this story? Is he going to be a
   student again? Write about him.